44 Routines
That Make a Difference

Strategies for the Effective Classroom

D0976552

School Renaissance Institute, Inc.
Madison, Wisconsin

School Renaissance Institute
P.O. Box 45016
Madison, WI 53744-5016
(800) 200-4848

Printed in the United States of America

ISBN 1-893751-61-9

Writing and editing by Kraft & Kraft
Illustrations by George Sebok

Cover art: Special thanks to the following artists for drawings of their teachers. Top right: Timothy Hardie (Mrs. Hardie, grade 2); clockwise from center: Amanda Schwartz (Mrs. Thoman, grade 2); Adam Schwartz (Ms. Bushner, kindergarten); Joel MacDonald (Mrs. DeRubis, kindergarten); Daniel Anania (Mr. Herbert, grade 8); Ingrid Klyve-Madden (Mrs. Severa, Spanish, grade 8).

5/01

Contents

Managing Student Behavior

Ending Each Day—And the Year

Suggested Reading 65

Introduction

Effective classrooms have an important characteristic in common, as research tells us repeatedly: They have teachers who have established routines for getting daily tasks done. Routines create order and security for students. They minimize wasted time and confusion and reduce disruptions.

A routine is a procedure that has become automatic. Students know what to expect as well as what is expected of them. But routines don't just happen. They must be planned, taught, practiced, and reinforced—and taught again if necessary.

In a classroom with routines in place, things run smoothly. Work gets done. And the atmosphere is calm, not chaotic. The teacher can teach, and the students can learn. In a classroom without routines, students often are anxious. They don't know what to expect. Their frustration with the lack of organization may erupt into discipline problems, which take time away from teaching and learning.

Whether this is your first year of teaching or your fifteenth, we hope you'll find routines in this book that will improve your days in the classroom—and your students' days, too.

1 Designing Your Room Arrangement

Plan your room arrangement before school starts. Keep three considerations in mind: visibility, accessibility, distractibility.

- Sketch a simple diagram of your room on graph paper. Make cutouts to represent major pieces of furniture and dividers. Experiment with various arrangements.
- Suit the arrangement to the type of activities that students will be involved in most often.
- Be sure students can see the chalkboard and displays easily. Check to see that you can see every student clearly.
- Keep traffic areas clear of obstructions.
- Be sure students won't be distracted by sitting too close to doorways and windows.

2 Assigning Seats

At first, you may want to . . .

- assign students' desks by alphabetical order and have students find their seats by looking for name tags placed on each desk.
- use a matching game for younger students. For example, give students a colored shape when they enter the room. They find that same colored shape on their desks, such as a yellow square, a yellow circle, or a blue star.
- place a puzzle piece on each student's desk. (See page 6.)
- have students' names written on a seating chart transparency, which is projected onto the wall or a screen.
- have students choose any desk they wish (but be sure to tell them that you will be making desk assignments later).

After you observe how students respond to one another, you may want to . . .

- group students who work well together.
- separate students who are disruptive when they're together.
- pair students with complementary abilities so that they can help each other.

Also consider . . .

- whether some students need to be seated near you and/or the chalkboard so they can see or hear better.
- whether some students need closer supervision from you.

3 Dealing With Students' Belongings

If students don't have lockers, you'll want to provide another way they can keep their lunch boxes, backpacks, and outdoor clothing in order.

- ✏ Establish a storage area in an easily accessible part of the classroom. Make sure everyone has a good view of the area so that it is always under watch.
- ✏ Have an individual box for each student. Plastic boxes that lock into a grid are best because they can be arranged so that the open side faces outward. This will create a storage space—a cubbyhole, or "cubby"—for each student.
- ✏ Ask students to make name labels for their cubbies.
- ✏ Label one cubby for lost-and-found items.

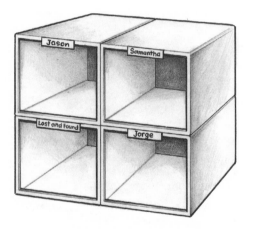

*Create individual storage spaces or "cubbies"
to organize students' belongings.*

4 Learning Students' Names: Create a Class Puzzle

So many unfamiliar faces. So many new names. How can you learn them all? One way is to have students wear name tags for the first week or so. Wear one yourself. You might also try the following puzzle or the nameplates on pages 8–9.

✏ Before school starts, make a large puzzle out of butcher paper. Write a student's name on each puzzle piece and cut the puzzle apart.

✏ On the first day of school, students find their puzzle piece on their desk. Have them write on it some things about themselves: names of family members and pets, favorite foods, music, hobbies.

✏ As a group activity, students put the puzzle together and attach it to the bulletin board. Title it "Our Class Belongs Together."

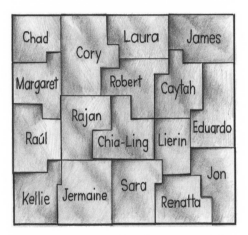

*Make a puzzle out of butcher paper to help
students learn classmates' names.*

5 Learning Students' Names: Make Nameplates

Ask students to make executive-style nameplates for their desks. These nameplates will continue to be useful long after you've learned all students' names. They're great for substitutes and to help volunteers return papers to the right desks.

- Nameplates can be made from construction paper folded and taped in the shape of a triangle so they will sit on the desk.
- Have students print their names clearly on one side of the triangle. First names are probably sufficient, with initials for last names as needed.
- You may want students to decorate their nameplates to show their individuality.
- Tape edges together when students have finished decorating.

Nameplates are easy to make—just fold and tape construction paper to form a triangle.

6 Getting Acquainted: Create an "Our Class" Bulletin Board

Remember the saying "A stranger is just a friend you haven't met"? Make an "Our Class" bulletin board to introduce students to one another.

- Have students choose a sheet of construction paper in a favorite color to label with their names, decorate, and post on a bulletin board. Make one for yourself, too. Now everyone has a personal space.
- Students can add clippings, drawings, or snapshots to their personal spaces. Encourage them to bring in personal items from home as well.
- Students could also make self-portraits, portraits of one another, or silhouettes for the personal spaces.
- Invite students to interview one another, write up their interviews, and include them on the spaces.

Students will enjoy decorating their personal spaces with clippings, drawings, and favorite items from home.

7 Getting Acquainted: Make Acrostics

Another way students can learn about one another is to make acrostics, using the letters of their names.

- ✎ Make an acrostic for your name and post it on a bulletin board. Use words or phrases for each letter that reveal some things about you.
- ✎ Have students make acrostics of their names as well. They write the letters of their names vertically. Then they use each letter of the name to begin a word or phrase that tells about themselves.
- ✎ Invite students to present their acrostics to the class by telling more about each word or phrase they've written.

Invite students to make acrostics of their names,
using words and phrases that tell about themselves.

8

Using the Class List

It seems like a simple thing, but your class list is a great asset. Make several copies and always keep them handy. Use them to organize classroom procedures and delegate tasks. They're also great any time you need to make notes next to students' names, such as:

- transportation arrangements
- attendance
- grouping for special projects
- parent conferences
- completion of long-term projects
- daily participation
- lunch count
- homework turned in
- classroom job assignments

9   Using Name Cards

Use sets of name cards to streamline many management tasks without resorting to numbering students.

- Have each student make several name cards, using 3-by-5-inch index cards. Encourage students to decorate their cards to individualize them.

- Use the cards to group students for teams, activities, or projects. Shuffle the cards to group students at random, or deal the cards onto a table and move them into groups as you wish.

- At the start of each day, shuffle a stack of cards and leave it on a corner of your desk. As you go through the day, whenever you want to choose a student to respond or give someone a turn, draw the top card. This ensures that all students get involved during the course of the day.

10 Delegating Jobs to Students

You can't do it all on your own—and there's no need to. Students love to do many of the routine tasks in the classroom, freeing you for other matters. Jobs you may want to delegate include:

- taking attendance
- collecting and distributing papers
- taking lunch count
- watering plants
- setting up audio-visual equipment
- tending the classroom library
- feeding the class pet

Remember that you will need to teach students how to do the jobs that you delegate to them.

You may want to make a jobs bulletin board, using students' name cards and pictures. Connect name cards to job titles with colorful yarn. Change names on the board each week.

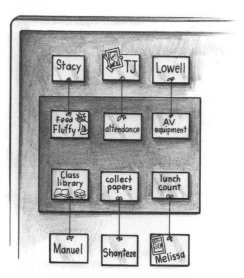

A jobs bulletin board will help organize your classroom tasks. Give it pizzazz with pictures and colorful yarn.

11 Establishing a Mail Center

If you establish a mail center in your class-room, you can encourage interaction in an orderly fashion. A note passed between students during class is a disruption, but a letter posted through the mail center is an exercise in written communication.

- To create mailboxes, use cardboard cartons with internal separators, like those that hold beverage bottles. Papers will need to be rolled up, but these boxes require little space in the classroom.
- Be sure to include a mailbox for yourself. Students can use it for suggestions (such as for field trips) and special requests (for a read-aloud book).
- Use students' boxes for notices to parents, return of graded papers, and written interaction with students.

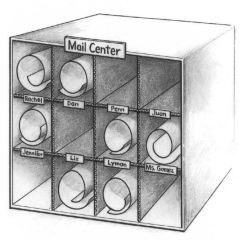

A mail center can be as simple as a cardboard box with separators.

12 Using a Class Newsletter

Keep in touch! A newsletter keeps parents informed and involves them in students' learning. You can use a computer to give your newsletter professional polish, but even a simple handwritten newsletter can alert parents to:

- forms to be completed and returned
- long-term student projects
- upcoming tests
- what students are currently studying
- ways that parents can help their children at home
- classroom needs (both materials and assistance)

If you start a newsletter, publish it regularly. Once a week is best; twice monthly works, too. Parents will come to rely on it to keep them informed.

13   Using an Opening Assignment

When the day begins, there is much to be done. While you are concentrating on morning administrative tasks, such as taking attendance and collecting permission slips, some students will be bored and may become unruly if they are not occupied.

- Get students involved in learning from the moment they arrive in the room by writing a question or activity on the board before class. Plan to grade or record this activity so students take it seriously and know they are responsible for completing it.
- Activities might include:
  - a math problem
  - a word of the day to be defined and used in writing
  - a focusing question you will return to in a later lesson, such as, "What do you think about . . ."

14

Taking Attendance: Use an "In-Out" Chart

Recording attendance should take as little time as possible and can be done while students are working on an opening assignment. (See page 21.)

✐ Create an "In-Out" Chart, using library book pockets. Label each pocket with a student's name. Keep a supply of colored paper slips beside the chart. Every morning, students put slips into their chart pockets to indicate they are "in." At the end of the day, or whenever they leave the room, they remove their slips to indicate they are "out."

Other suggestions for taking attendance:

✐ Ask a student to take attendance, using a copy of the class list.
✐ Have students sign in on an attendance sheet that is always posted in the same place.

One glance at this chart tells you who is "in" and who is "out."

15

Taking Attendance:
Use an Attendance/Lunch Chart

You can expand the "In-Out" Chart (pages 22–23) to include lunch count as well.

✏ Use the same pockets labeled with students' names. Supply several colors of paper slips so students can signify their daily lunch choices: For example, red—hot lunch; brown—brown bag lunch; orange—hot dog; white—milk only.

✏ When students arrive each day, they put colored slips into their chart pockets to indicate not only that they are "in" but also what they want for lunch. Since the lunch count is taken early in the morning, students can still remove the slips when they leave the room to show they are "out."

16 Dealing With Tardiness

Tardiness may seem like a small matter, but if you allow it to persist it can send the message that you're not serious about rules. Set a tardiness policy (or inform students of the school's policy) and then follow it to the letter. Be sure to mark tardiness as you would absence.

- Keep a record of students' tardiness. If you have students sign in when they arrive, you can have them mark themselves tardy if they are late. Keep a notebook or clipboard near the door. Tardy students should still sign in before sitting down.
- If students have written excuses for being late, they should leave them in a designated spot when they arrive. They should *not* interrupt class to give them to you.

17   Teaching Classroom Procedures

At the beginning of the year, you may want to jump right into teaching content, but establishing procedures first will build a base from which you can teach effectively throughout the year. Plan to spend time during the first two weeks teaching procedures. Spending time this way will pay dividends throughout the school year.

It's best to start teaching procedures on the first day of school. Actually *teach* them, don't just *tell* them. You may want to try this simple three-step process:

✎ Explain: Define the procedure and tell why it's needed. Then demonstrate it for students—exaggerate and use humor to make your point.

✎ Practice: Go through each procedure with students and have them repeat the procedure until it becomes a routine.

- Reinforce: Tell students how they're doing. Give positive feedback when procedures are performed correctly and helpful feedback when procedures need to be corrected.

You may need procedures for:

- getting students' attention
- taking attendance
- use of the room and equipment
- individual work, whole-class, and group activities
- transitions between activities and to and from other locations
- beginning and ending the day
- distributing and collecting materials

18 Posting Schedules

Give the day and week a structure and rhythm students can depend on. A predictable pattern shows students what to expect and what you expect of them. For example, they will know they should be ready for a spelling test every Friday.

- Make weekly and daily schedules and post them prominently. For the first two or three weeks, refer to the charts at the beginning of each day—and from time to time throughout each day—to accustom students to the idea that the plans for the day and week are on the charts.
- Use a format that can be changed and adjusted, such as a section of the chalkboard, a whiteboard, or cards pinned to a bulletin board.

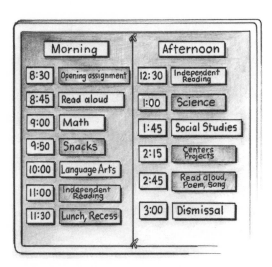

Weekly and daily schedules help students know what to expect.

19 Providing Variety

A restaurant's regular menu is predictable and comforting to regular clientele, but a wise chef supplements it with specials to provide some variety.

Similarly, predictable daily and weekly classroom schedules provide stability and structure, but they can become dull if they are repeated without variation. Surprise specials are stimulating. Providing variety keeps interest high. So, offer daily and weekly "specials" within the schedule, such as:

- guest speakers
- "science in the news" bulletins
- crossword puzzles or other games
- breaks for painting or music
- pen-pal correspondence

	Monday	Tuesday	Wednesday
8:00	Opening Assignment	Opening Assignment	Opening Assignment
8:15	Read aloud: Harriet the Spy	Read aloud: Harriet the Spy	Read aloud: Harriet the Spy
8:30	Language Arts	Language Arts	★Language Arts "Wheel of Fortune" Spelling
9:30	Science	Science ★ Guest: Ms. Chaney "Chemistry" Is a Blast!	Science

Students need a regular schedule, but they love surprise specials for some variety, too.

20 Using Show-and-Tell With Themes

Show-and-tell is a wonderful way for young students to develop oral language skills. If you're tired of seeing the same dolls and toys presented with little forethought, link show-and-tell with your themes.

- Invite students to share on a weekly basis, even if your themes last longer than that. Items can be very simple, such as a picture of a car, cut from a magazine, for a transportation theme. Students may also tell about an experience related to the theme, rather than showing an object.
- Because parents often help children with show-and-tell items, let them know about upcoming themes well in advance. Your class newsletter is a great way to communicate! (See page 20.)

21   Getting Students' Attention

You will need a way to get students' attention while they are working before a lesson begins. Choose a procedure that suits you and practice it with students so it becomes a routine.

- Ring a small hand bell.
- Raise your hand without speaking.
- Put your finger to your lips to indicate "silence."
- Use "Give Me Five." When you raise one hand and say "Give me five," students follow the five steps shown.

  1. Look at the teacher.
  2. Be quiet.
  3. Be still.
  4. Put things down.
  5. Listen.

- Every morning, write an intriguing vocabulary word on the chalkboard, always in the same place. Use that word as the attention-getting signal for the day.

22 Using Materials and Equipment

Establish procedures for using materials and equipment and for special-activity areas of the classroom.

- Demonstrate the use of every piece of equipment students will use. Then have them practice under your supervision before they use it on their own.
- Attach rules and instructions for use of equipment to the items themselves.
- In each activity area, post rules and procedures for use. For example:
  - an occupancy limit telling how many students may use the materials or equipment at one time
  - a sign-up sheet for determining who is next in line to use the equipment

23   Distributing Materials

The trick to distributing materials efficiently is to keep the process from becoming a disruption. One or more of these procedures may work for you:

- Place materials on students' desks before class starts or before students return from an out-of-room activity.
- Use one or more student helpers to distribute materials.
- Use the mail center if you have established one. (See pages 18–19.)
- Designate one student in each row as the distributor for that row. Place a stack of papers on that student's desk and have her pass them across the row. For other materials, have the distributors get sufficient supplies for their rows and deliver them.

24 Conducting Seatwork Activities

These procedures will help keep students focused on work they do individually at their desks:

- Begin the activity with the whole class. Complete several problems or answer several questions together. Invite questions.
- Remind students of the established procedure for seeking help during an activity. (See page 38.)
- Be sure students have a copy of the assignment to refer to as they work. Write it on the chalkboard or duplicate it as a handout.
- Then have students complete the assignment by themselves.
- Have options for early finishers, such as reading for pleasure, helping others, or using the computer.

25 Asking Questions

Generally it's a good idea to ask a question before calling on a student to answer it. Asking first requires all students to pay attention since they don't know who you will call on.

- Give plenty of wait time—wait at least five seconds after asking a question before calling on a student or answering it yourself. This gives students time to think.
- Do not consistently repeat students' answers. If you do, students will pay attention only to you, rather than to other students' responses.
- Keep track to ensure that all students are called on with the same frequency. Student name cards are a handy method. (See page 15.)

26 Students' Obtaining Help

When students need help with seatwork, they should ask one another before seeking help from you. This policy ensures that you will be available for more serious difficulties students are having. One of these ideas may work for you:

- Teach students the 3B4ME ("three before me") procedure. A student should ask three other students for help before asking you.

- When students are working at their seats and need assistance, have them use "Help" cards. Fold construction paper to form a triangle. Label one side, "Please help me" and another side "Please keep working." As students need help, they turn the card so "Please help me" faces forward. They see "Please keep working" and are reminded to continue working until you arrive to help them.

Using "Help" cards is one way students can signal that they need your assistance.

27 Choosing Teams or Forming Groups

When you group students for projects, you may be tempted to set group size to any number that divides the class equally. A better idea is to base the size of each group on the requirements of the activity. These procedures will allow you to group students quickly and fairly:

✏ If you have a stack of student name cards prepared (see page 15), shuffle the stack and deal the cards into a number of piles corresponding to the number of teams or groups you need.

✏ Have students line up and count off by the number of students per group. (To count off by threes, for example, the first student calls out *one*, the second *two*, the third *three*, the fourth *one*, and so on.) Group students with the same number.

28 Working in Groups

Students want and need opportunities to work with others. Experts tell us that learning is often best achieved when kids can talk among themselves.

- Try to form heterogeneous groups if possible. Include high, average, and low achievers; girls and boys; different ethnic groups; and students with disabilities.
- Give certificates or other simple rewards when teams achieve at or above criteria.
- Be sure there is individual accountability. Team members will help one another with the work, but make it clear that each needs to complete a quiz or other assessment individually.
- Base part of the team's grade on individual improvement over previous work. In this way, students of all abilities are challenged to do their best.

29   Collecting Students' Work

One or more of the following procedures will
help you collect work with a minimum of
fuss and disruption.

- Have students put homework on a designated corner of your desk or on their
  desks when they arrive in the morning.
- Have students pass in-class papers across
  rows. Passing papers across rows rather
  than up columns allows you to observe
  the passing and helps prevent distur-
  bances. (Keep the papers in the same
  order while you are checking them. Then
  you can return them easily by giving
  groups to a distributor in each row.)
- Use the mail center, if you have established one. (See page 18.)

30 Making Up Work After Absence

If you give a homework assignment orally, it may be forgotten after you finish speaking. Instead, write the assignment on a sheet of paper and post it—always in the same place—on a bulletin board. These ideas will also help with make-up work:

- Maintain a loose-leaf binder with past assignments. Just punch each day's assignment sheet and insert it in the back of the binder. Keep the binder in an accessible place so that students who have been absent can find out what assignments they owe.
- Alternatively, designate a student to record assignments in a notebook. (Be sure to designate a backup in case this student is absent.)

When absent students return, they obtain their work from the binder or notebook, not from you.

31   Making Transitions Between Activities

Keep the loss of learning time to a minimum during transitions by letting students know what is expected—and what they can expect.

- If you have a posted schedule (see pages 28–29), review it at the start of each activity so students know when the activity will end.
- Give students notice before an activity ends. Tell them:
  - how to end the activity
  - what to do in the transition
  - when to be ready to begin the next activity
  - what to do to prepare for the next activity
- Don't begin the next activity until the transition is completed.

32 Walking Through the Hallway

Establish a procedure for moving from the classroom to other areas of the school, such as the lunchroom. Teach and practice the procedure before it is needed. For example:

- ✐ Ahead of time, find several "stopping points" in the hallway between your classroom and various destinations, such as a doorway or the top of a stairway.
- ✐ When it's time to go somewhere, students line up double file in the classroom or just outside the doorway.
- ✐ Two students are the leaders. They proceed through the hallway, stopping at each designated point until others catch up.
- ✐ You will want to walk with the group toward the middle of the line so you can watch all students.
- ✐ Continue in this way until the destination is reached.

33 Returning to the Classroom

When students return from an excursion outside the classroom, they are often excited and talkative. You will need a way to help them settle down and return to the work of the day.

✏ Involve them in a calming activity when they return to the room. One of the best is reading aloud. Establish a tradition of reading a high-interest book, episode by episode. If you choose a mystery with cliffhangers, students will look forward to finding out what happens next.

✏ You can turn to the book any time you need to refocus students' attention—after a fire drill, for example. You can also turn to it when there is time to fill—while waiting for a faulty overhead projector to be repaired, for example.

34 Individuals' Leaving the Room

This is a classic disruption—but you can control it. From time to time, students will need to leave the room individually. Establish a procedure to distinguish requests to leave from volunteering to answer a question. Here are several ideas:

- Give each student a token, such as a colored square of paper, to keep throughout the year and hold up to ask to leave the room. (Keep plenty of spares.)
- Have students use a distinctive hand signal (such as a "thumbs-up") to ask to leave the room.
- Use a hall pass. A laminated card with your name and room number will do the trick.
- If you have an "In-Out" procedure (see pages 22–23), have students use it whenever they leave the room.

35 Establishing Classroom Rules

Set the tone for a well-managed classroom right at the start of the year by letting students know what you expect. Whether you use general or specific rules, keep the number to five or fewer so they're easier for students to remember.

Some examples of general rules:
- Be polite.
- Be helpful.
- Respect other people's property.
- Listen while others are speaking.
- Follow all school rules.

Some examples of specific rules:
- Be on time.
- Keep hands, feet, and objects to yourself.
- Have materials ready.
- Stay seated.
- Listen to instructions.

Post the rules prominently, but don't stop there; teach the rules in a lesson format.

- Explain why the rules are necessary.
- Demonstrate expected behavior. You may want to model appropriate and inappropriate behavior—ham it up so kids will remember.
- Provide feedback to students and let them know the consequences of breaking the rules. (See pages 50–51.)
- Review the rules as needed throughout the year.

36 Imposing Conseqences for Violating Rules

Establish a ladder of escalating consequences for problem behavior. When you teach the classroom rules, discuss the consequences of breaking them.

- ✏ One way to handle minor problems is to keep a tally on a section of the chalkboard. Use check marks for rule violations and minutes of detention, time-out, or time lost from recess as consequences. Everyone begins the week with a clean slate, and everyone's name is erased at the end of the week.
- ✏ Post your consequences in a prominent place in the classroom.
- ✏ If you'd rather not go public with students' names on the board, keep the same tally on a clipboard on your desk. Inform students individually of rule violations and consequences.

Consequences

1st time:	Name on board	Warning
2nd time:	✓	15 minutes
3rd time:	✓✓	30 minutes
4th time:	✓✓✓	45 minutes Parent Called
5th time:	✓✓✓✓	60 minutes Student to Office

You may choose to keep a behavior tally on the chalkboard or in a more private place, such as on a clipboard on your desk.

37 Preventing Behavior Problems

It's an old, old saying, but it's true: An ounce of prevention is worth a pound of cure. If you take steps to *prevent* behavior problems, you will spend less time *dealing* with behavior problems.

- Keep students involved in meaningful work. Make seatwork engaging and challenging. Post a list of activities for early finishers: independent reading, computer time, exploration centers.
- Every student has a passion. If a difficult student loves horses, make horses the subject of an ongoing research project and invite the student to report periodically to the class.
- Be consistent about enforcing procedures and rules. And periodically review your rules and consequences.
- Monitor the classroom at all times. Know what's going on by scanning the room.

38 Managing Minor Behavior Problems

When unacceptable behavior occurs, end it as quickly as possible so that productive time is not lost and the behavior does not spread. Following is a list of progressive interventions:

- Make the student aware that you are aware. Make eye contact with the student, signal for silence with a finger to the lips, or shake your head.
- Move closer to the student.
- Calmly remind the student of the rule that is being broken or the procedure that is not being followed.
- Direct the student back to the task at hand: "You need to be working on your math now."
- Point out that the student is about to cross the line into consequences for inappropriate behavior. (See pages 50–51.)

39 Maintaining Good Behavior Throughout the Year

Too often, we think of managing behavior in terms of controlling or punishing inappropriate behavior. Actually, it is a balancing act. Success depends equally on encouraging appropriate behavior and discouraging inappropriate behavior.

- First, be sure that students understand what appropriate behavior is. Reward appropriate behavior as often as is practical. Tangible rewards are not necessary— praise works wonders.
- Second, be sure that students understand what inappropriate behavior is. Always stop inappropriate behavior promptly. Severe punishments are usually not necessary. Disapproval is a strong deterrent.

40 Closing Activities

Don't let the day end in a rush, with the day's accomplishments quickly forgotten and the homework assignment overlooked. Instead, use the last quarter hour to reinforce the learning that has taken place.

- End activities fifteen minutes before the end of the school day.
- Have students sit quietly in their seats. Give them—and yourself—a chance to relax.
- Review the day's activities.
- Preview tomorrow's activities.
- Draw attention to the posted homework assignment.
- Remind students about any messages they should take home.
- Conclude the day with a song or a short reading, such as a poem or fable.

Posting Homework Assignments

Avoid giving a homework assignment orally only. Some students will not hear it correctly, some will catch only part of it, and some will forget it.

☞ Write the assignment on the chalkboard or on a sheet of paper and post it on a bulletin board—always in the same designated place. (Keeping past assignments in a loose-leaf binder will allow students who have been absent to find out what assignments they owe. See page 43.)

☞ Every homework assignment should include the following elements:
  – the assignment itself
  – the purpose of the assignment
  – clear directions
  – a list of materials needed, if any, including textbooks
  – the due date

It's important for students to record the homework assignments you've posted. Otherwise they may forget the instructions or necessary details. One of these suggestions may work for your students:

- Have students keep an assignment notebook to record the assignment and its due date.
- Have students write the assignment on the first line of their paper before they take it home.
- Prepare a weekly homework sheet and give a copy to each student. Make an overhead transparency to use as a template. At the end of each day, students record their assignments as you write them on your transparency.

Monday (Date)	Tuesday (Date)
Language Arts_____	Language Arts_____
Math_____	Math_____
Science_____	Science_____
Social Studies_____	Social Studies_____

42

Sending Materials Home: Use Fabric Squares

Messages and forms that students are supposed to take home will have a better chance of making it there if you follow a procedure. Here is one suggestion. See pages 60–61 for another.

- Cut enough small squares of yellow and red fabric for the class and attach a safety pin to each one.

- When you distribute messages to students, distribute the squares of fabric, too. Use yellow for messages that don't have to be returned, red for forms that have to be completed and returned.

- Have students pin the fabric to their backpacks or clothing to remind themselves (and signal their parents) that they have a message.

- Staple a copy of any form that must be returned to a copy of your class list. Check students' names as forms are returned.

- Be sure to keep extra copies of forms. Some dogs *will* eat them.

Fabric squares remind students—and signal their parents—about messages from school.

43 Sending Materials Home: Use Manila Envelopes

This suggestion may work best for younger students who would have difficulty using safety pins, as noted in the suggestion on page 58.

- ✎ Send messages home in a sturdy, reusable manila envelope labeled with the student's name.
- ✎ Tape or staple a signature sheet on the front that includes a place for the date and the number of papers you're sending home.
- ✎ Put a red *X* at the top of all papers that must be signed and returned.

For younger students, send materials home in a reusable manila envelope.

44 Over the Summer

Address four envelopes to each student, indicating the date each should be opened. Space the dates out evenly over the summer. In each envelope, describe an activity that will keep learning alive during the vacation, such as:

- a suggestion of things to find out during a visit to a library
- a simple science experiment or observation
- a suggested reading list of high-interest, "just for fun" books
- pencil-and-paper games, such as crossword puzzles and word searches
- an invitation to write a letter to next year's students, telling them about your class and what to expect in it, such as rules, procedures, high points of the year, and favorite readings. Students can give you these during the first week of the new school year.

Keep the learning alive! Stimulate students'
interests with activities for summer fun.

Suggested Reading

Emmer, E.T., et al. (1997). *Classroom management for secondary teachers.* Boston: Allyn and Bacon.

Evertson, C.M., et al. (1997). *Classroom management for elementary teachers.* Boston: Allyn and Bacon.

Evertson, C.M. (1987). Managing classrooms: A framework for teachers. In Berliner, D. & Rosenshine, B., eds. (1987). *Talks to teachers.* New York: Random House.

Slavin, R.E. (1994). *A practical guide to cooperative learning.* Boston: Allyn and Bacon.

Walmsley, B.B., Camp, A.M., & Walmsley, S.A. (1992). *Teaching kindergarten: A developmentally appropriate approach.* Portsmouth, NH: Heinemann.

Wong, H.K. & Wong, R.T. (1998). *The first days of school.* Mountain View, CA: Harry K. Wong Publications, Inc.

Small Books
with BIG Ideas
for Teachers!

Life-Saving Strategies for New Teachers

This small book contains the practical, specific tips and techniques that new teachers need to know—and usually learn only through hard experience. You'll find out how to have a great first day, prevent discipline problems, communicate with parents, and lots more.

ISBN 1-893751-88-0
Item #TS15-3153 $8.95
**Mix and match! Order 10 or more
of either book and save! Only $7.95.**

44 Routines That Make a Difference: Strategies for the Effective Classroom

This small book of routines will make a BIG difference in your classroom right away! You'll learn effective new ways to take attendance, give assignments, collect homework, and deal with behavior problems, creating a smooth-running classroom where students learn more!

ISBN 1-893751-61-9
Item #TS15-3088 $8.95
**Mix and match! Order 10 or more
of either book and save! Only $7.95.**

Order Today!
Phone: (800) 200-4848, Dept. 4184
Fax: (800) 295-4985
Web: www.SchoolRenaissance.com
Mail: School Renaissance Institute
PO Box 45016
Madison, WI 53744-5016

School
Renaissance™
Institute

Order form on back. →

Order Today!

Item No.	Quantity	Price Each[†]	Amount
1.			
2.			

†Mix and match, order 10 or more and pay only $7.95 each!

Order Total	Shipping
Up to $49.99	$4.95
$50.00 to $249.99	$7.95
$250.00 to $449.99	$12.95

*Books are taxable in Calif., La., N.C., and S.C.
Call (800) 200-4848 for more information.

+ Shipping _____

Subtotal _____

Sales Tax* _____

TOTAL _____

Ship To: (Please use street address only)

Name _____

Title _____Grade(s) _____

School/District _____

Street Address _____

City _____ State _____ ZIP _____

Phone (____) _____

Method of Payment:

❑ Check enclosed (payable to School Renaissance™ Institute)

❑ Bill my school (purchase order required**) P.O. # _____

❑ Bill my district (purchase order required**) P.O. # _____

❑ MasterCard® ❑ VISA® ❑ Discover® ❑ American Express®

The following information is required for credit card orders:

Account No. _____

Exp. Date _____

Signature _____

Home Phone (____) _____

** You may mail or fax us a fully executed purchase order with approved number. Purchase orders are billed net 30 days. Sorry, we cannot accept oral purchase orders.

Pricing Information: All prices are F.O.B. Madison, Wis. Prices are effective January 1, 2001, and are subject to change without notice.

Warranty/Replacement: Books are guaranteed to be free from defects in materials and workmanship. School Renaissance Institute will replace books found to be defective.